Selah!
PAUSE AND REFLECT

Sharon Dexter

Copyright © 2024 **Sharon Dexter Publishing**

All rights reserved. No part of this publication may be reproduced, distributed, or transmitted in any form or by any means, including photocopying, recording, or other electronic or mechanical methods, without the prior written permission of the publisher, except in the case of brief quotations embodied in critical reviews and certain other noncommercial uses permitted by copyright law. For permission requests, write to the publisher, addressed "Attention: Book Rights and Permission," at the address below.

Published in the United States of America

ISBN 978-1-960684-00-4 (SC)
ISBN 978-1-960159-29-8 (Ebook)

Sharon Dexter Publishing
222 West 6th Street
Suite 400, San Pedro, CA, 90731
godsfaithfulpromise.com

Order Information and Rights Permission:

Quantity sales. Special discounts might be available on quantity purchases by corporations, associations, and others. For details, contact the publisher at the address above.

For Book Rights Adaptation and other Rights Permission. Call us at toll-free 1-888-945-8513 or send us an email at admin@stellarliterary.com.

Contents

Beginning: You Were There

You Were There 2

Beginning: to Think

Judgement 4
Where Are the Children 5
Do I? 6
Why Church? 7
Wow! How do I begin? 8
Accountable 9
Don't Be a Fool 10
Don't 11
Merely 12
Why Did I Come? 13
Do Good 14
Bombarded 15
Pray Now 16
Remember 17
What Works 18
The Remnant 19
It's Not Always Easy 20
Don't Be Stupid 21
In the Interim 22
Unlikely Heroes 23
Moses 24
My Barriers 25
Learn to Listen 26
Stay Alert 27
Your Peace Restored 28
Conversations 29
Acquitted 30

Goliath	31
Different	32
Say "Ahhhh"	33
A Sin	34
A Remnant	35
Awareness of Presence	36
The Loser	37
Lost Time	38
In Holy Presence	39
God Calls	40
Heart-Faith	41
What's Your Answer	42
The Thirsty Earth	43
End or Beginning	44

A Bit Deeper

The Cross	46
Don't Just Sit	47
Do Not Doubt	48
Another Experience	49
Move Forward	50
Time to Repent	51
For You	52
Priority One	53
Me	54
The Reason	55
How Dare I?	56
The Shape of Waiting	57
Don't Even Try	58
January First	59
Jesus First	60
As God Said	61
Jesus Asked Me	62
Half Enough	63
Insulted	64
Risk	65

The Waters	66
Aimless	67
Prepare the Way	68
A Turned-On Believer	69
For This Delights Him	70
Life Answers	71
Death—Life	72
God's Acceptance	73
Jesus Rules	74
You Are My God	75
Rest Restores	76
My Lines	77
God's Poem	78
Be Still and Know	79
Ponder Impossible	80
Indispensable Weapon	81
Lord, You Save Me	82
My Life as Prayer	83
The Lord	84
What Joy	85
Who Do You Say I Am?	86
Invited	87
Make Your Choice	88
The Next Moment	89
Best Friends	90
We, Your People	91
God vs. Satan	92
Who Upset the World?	93
Doubt	94
I Can't Understand	95
The Lord's Call	96
Truth	97
Daddy, Would You Come	98
Do For	99
Your Mercy and Grace	100
Paul	101

Hard Times or Good	102
Be Prepared	103
Two Other Crosses	104
Gifts I Bear	105
His Faithful Love	106
Hope, Joy, and Happiness	107
I Will Serve	108
You Hem Me In	109
In the Now	110
God's Gifts	111
Before It Began	112
Egypt	113
Foundation of Grace	114
The Will	115
Share the Blessing	116
Lush and Lovely	117
The Design	118
Joy of the Lord	119
My Last Breath	120
The Empty Tomb	121
Faithful	122
Gifts	123
Looking Back	124
Hush, Child, Hush	125
Music of Heaven	126
Handcrafted	127
No Darkness	128
Amen	129

A Bit Deeper

At Home with God	131

Beginning: You Were There

You Were There

You were there to hear my cry at birth,
You are there throughout my life.
You'll be there to hear my sigh at death,
As I relinquish love and strife.
You will hold me in Your tender arms,
You will kiss my fevered brow.
You will love me, Lord, eternally,
Just as You love me now.

Beginning to think

Judgement

In judgment for their wicked ways,
The Lord let loose the hordes of men
Against His people,
For they had turned their backs on Him,
And made their vows to other gods.
Therefore, judgment came.

Where Are the Children

Where are the children—
    The girls of Nigeria
    Stolen for pleasure
    Of somebody else?
Where are the children—
    Sent over our borders
    Bearing resentments
    Of somebody else?
Where are the children—
    Those in the big cities
    Hurting from shootings
    Of somebody else?
Where are the children—
    Of good Christian families,
    Yet selling the drugs
    To somebody else?
Where are God's people—
    Those God-fearing people?
    Cleaning the messes
    For "somebody" else

Do I?

I have an acquaintance.
We were introduced earlier tonight.
He sure looks tired, maybe even drunk.
Oh? Up all night, you say?
With a sick baby?
Sorry, I didn't know.

I have a friendly acquaintance.
We've worked together for years now.
I think she's been on an extended vacation this month.
Oh? She's been in the hospital?
Rehab after surgery?
Sorry, I hadn't known.

I have a really good friend.
We practically grew up together.
I've tried to set her up with blind dates.
Oh? She had an abusive father?
She's afraid of men?
Really? I'd never realized!

Well, surely, I know my God!
I go to church every Sunday.
He created everything, you know.
Oh? He wants more of me than attending?
You mean, like a personal commitment?

Why Church?

I've gone to services
    For all my life,
    From five days old 'til now.
Surely, I can worship
    Alone, in quiet privacy.
I'm a good person.
    I follow all the rules.
Why do I need church?
    Others need it much more than I.
    Church just isn't for everyone.

I beg to differ.
Others also embody Christ
    With their presence, their song,
The touch, and concerns of love
    Permeate their worship.
As we hear, see, touch Christ
    We become more aware
    Of God's holy presence
    In them,
        And in ourselves.
As we grow in our own relationship
    With God and with other Christians,
We also become
    The "Presence of God"
        In the world.
In worship, we bond,
    And are transformed,
    To obedience to His will.
Alone, we are stuck
    With only our own interpretations…
Assuming, of course,
    We actually bother to try to interpret.

Wow! How do I begin?

Lord, expose my false security,
Deepen my knowledge, my understanding of Your way.
Lord, I believe. Help Thou mine unbelief.
Oh, pull the weeds from my heart, Lord.
Replant the roots of my faith,
Deep into the rich soil of Your love.

Accountable

I am held accountable
For each action, and each inaction,
I have done or left undone.
Yet, in repenting
I am forgiven.
In His mercy, He restores me.

Though at the Day of Judgment
I will be held accountable,
I'll not abandon the hope
That in His courtroom
I'll be forgiven,
For Jesus has paid for my sins.

Don't Be a Fool

You say there is no God?
Don't be a fool!
If God does not exist,
Then who has made the stars?
Who caused the dawn to know its place?
Who calls forth the wind?

Have you never read His word?
Try it, and you will find Him.
It was God who led the Israelites
Through the Red Sea
And beyond the desert
Into the Promised Land.
It was God, in Jesus Christ,
Who gave up His place in heaven
To live among His people.
He who performed those miracles,
And willingly gave His life—
For you!

Have you never read His word?
Try it, and you will find Him!
Ask Him, just ask Him
To open your eyes.
He will open your heart as well.

Don't

Don't be "things oriented,"
    Don't be "me, my, I!"
Don't be dominated by
    Your wants, desires, or riches!
Don't ignore each other,
    But most of all, remember,
        Do *not*
            Ignore
                Your God!

Merely

Merely folding my hands,
And bowing my head,
Even to press palms
Against my forehead,
Though it may *seem* to be,
This posture is not praying.

Merely reading Your Word,
Seeking Your presence
Each morning at dawn
And at eventide;
If I do not obey,
I'm not *living* Your presence.

If I *truly* believe,
Then will I worship,
Give thanks for blessings.
Merely pretending
Won't bring me home to You,
In heaven—where I belong.

Why Did I Come?

Why did I come to church today?
Am I attending because it is Sunday,
    And my friends are there,
    And it is "expected" of me?
Am I attending because of my need;
    Do I need others to affirm me?
    Do I need to receive God's blessings,
    But heard, "If you give, you'll receive"?
Or do I come to church to worship?
    Knowing how much You love me, Lord,
    I must respond in kindness
    And show love to others.
Facing Your altar in worship,
    Joined with other like-minded souls,
    Together we reaffirm Your love for us, and ours for You.
    Your holy sacrifice we celebrate through communion.
Leaving Your Holy House, we realize,
    The next step is up to us.
    Will we remain open to You during the week?
    Will our actions reflect Your glory?
    Will we live our love of You, Lord?
    Will we live our faith?

Do Good

I was almost satisfied
But, it felt like something was missing.
I'd done a pretty good job—
The best possible, with what I had.
But a "good job" wasn't requested.
He'd said, "My child, do good."

I read my Bible, daily.
I prayed, nearly every single day.
But still, something was missing.
My life, my heart, felt dim and grimy.
And then, I heard my Savior repeat,
"My child, I said, do good."

Lord, what do You *want* of me?
When I attempt to feed the hungry,
There are always more in need.
I'm unable to reach every one
Who seem to need a soft, loving touch
What do You *mean*, "Do good"?

"Just do whatever you can,
Wherever you are needed to serve.
Feed the hungry you can see;
When you have an extra coat, give one.
I ask that you will help another.
To serve Me, child, *do good*."

Bombarded

Is there a moral decline in society?
Is there no longer a sense of propriety?
Are we interested in an opportunity
To show ourselves as a Christian,
Yet, not be completely shot down?
Since I'm called by God to live in society,
How can I so live, Lord, when I am bombarded?

Pray Now

Don't wait for troubles
To show up on your own doorstep
Before you get down
On your knees, in prayer.

I beg you, pray *now*!
Prayer is delight for the joyful,
Surrounding others
With God's strength and love.

Prayer is a request
That may or may not be granted.
Ask God for guidance
Of His will for you.

Please, don't be silent
Before Him, the God of your heart,
For rocks will cry out
If You don't praise Him!

Remember

A child, rattling papers,
Distracted me from prayer.
Angry, I turned to glare.
Then, remembering the times
My mind rattled about
When nothing distracted me,
I smiled at him instead.

Many distractions vie,
Daily, for attention,
Attempt to keep me from You.
But You will be my Guide,
And I'll not be shaken.
I'll remember to focus…
Then, God will smile at me.

What Works

Are you living on "Spiritual fast food,"
Never noticing the great banquet
God, Himself, has prepared for you?
How is that working for you?

Do you just survive with "drive-through" service,
Reading devotions when you "have time,"
Not planning for the time or place?
Does that truly work for you?

I prefer sitting and reading the Word
Every morning when I first arise.
Otherwise, I'd often forget,
And that will *not* work for me!

If I have a plan before the crisis,
Then I'm more prepared for anything
The world of evil produces.
That way, God's working *with* me!

The Remnant

Can you not see;
Is your heart insensitive
To His holy presence?
Will you be of the "other,"
Or a part of the "Remnant"?
Are you ready to see Him
Face-to-face?

Did you compromise your faith
By "going along"
When evil beckoned?
Or had you been loyal,
Part of the "Remnant" of faith.
Know that nothing
Can defeat God's love!

It's Not Always Easy

It's not always easy
To be a paragon of virtue,
To believe everyone
Thinks you can never be mistaken!

It's not always easy
To be a model of perfection.
But then, You understand
The foibles of being merely man.

It's not always easy
To live without sin, knowing You're God;
For virtuous perfection—
To be crucified! *Never* "easy"!

Don't Be Stupid

Don't be a fool.
Don't be so stupid as to prefer a "black market substitute"
    For God!
You know what is wise and what is not,
So, don't be a fool,
    A stubborn, stupid fool!
Don't continue doing stupid things,
But change your ways.
    Decide for God.

But then again,
May I be "stupid" in the way of Jesus.
When tempted, after fasting,
    He continued in God's way.
We succumb—before temptations—
    To hunger and to thirst once again.
When tempted, offered power and prestige,
    He followed in His Father's way.

O Lord, may we be "stupid" as was Your Son!
May we follow Him: to live,
    To die, to overcome, as He.
Christ offers life—abundant and eternal.
I ask you: Who is so stupid
    As to refuse His plea?

In the Interim

Lord, I know, from past experiences,
All *will* be well indeed.
It is only in the interim
That we ask our questions.

In this dreary, weary land, O Lord,
Where I am now searching,
This, my "interim time," is so hard;
Your love seems far away.

In the darkness of my nighttime fears,
When sin looms over me,
Still, I realize all *will* be well
When Your light dawns again!

Unlikely Heroes

Moses made wrong choices.
He killed an overseer,
Ran off then to escape
The consequence of sin.
God chose this man to lead
His people home again.

Jonah made wrong choices.
He tried to sail away,
Storms threatened to destroy
And he's thrown overboard,
Was swallowed by the whale.
Then, followed God's request.

Peter made wrong choices.
Disciple of the Christ,
Yet still he went astray—
Denied his Lord—three times!
God chose this man to lead,
And feed His lambs on earth.

What choices have I made
That God can turn and use?
Have I heard His whisper?
And if He'd choose to use me,
I'd certainly become
An unlikely hero!

Moses

God came to the mountain
With smoke, fire, and earthquakes.
While trumpets were blasting,
With thunder, God called him,
"Moses, come, meet with Me."
    And Moses went.

If God spoke thus to me,
Would I even respond?
Would I shiver and shake
Instead of obeying?
    But, Moses went up!

The bravery of Abram
To go where God told him;
The bravery of Jacob
When offering Isaac;
    Is matched by Moses!

My Barriers

I designed a beautiful barrier
Between my Lord and myself.
Comprised of all those "religious" acts,
Embellished with those "feel-good" phrases,
It stood secure, for ages.

But lately, putting all trust in God
Revealed to me my error.
When I remember His promises,
To be with me in each circumstance,
I'll be secure forever.

So, I destroyed the barrier I'd built
Between my Lord and myself.
I tore it down, reseeded the soil.
I know I'll never need to rebuild,
For I'm secure without it!

Learn to Listen

Each time I speak has a consequence.
Whatever I say shows my heart.
If I speak ill of anyone,
I prove the evil within me.

And if I listen, there's consequence.
A quality of character
Is listening *before* speaking.
I will choose to listen to God.

How can I hear, and when does He speak?
He speaks through Holy, written Word.
Wanting to know the "good" within,
I'll learn to obey—to *listen*.

Stay Alert

Two factions live inside my heart,
The evil of the world will war
The Spirit's help within us.
"Stay alert! Keep watch, keep praying!"*
Don't allow the evil to rise,
But squelch its power over you
With grace of the Holy Spirit.

The good, Lord, that I want to do
Is at war with evil impulse.
Help me control my sins, O Lord,
Never allow control to slip,
Allowing entrance of the world
Into my heart to control me.
"Stay alert! Keep watch, keep praying!"*

*Mark 13:33, NLT

Your Peace Restored

May Your peace be restored.
In this nation of divided hearts,
Of divided loyalties, and divisive hatreds—
Oh Lord, may Your peace be restored!

In this world of evil intent,
Where brothers war against brothers,
Lord, we need You more than ever before!
May Your Peace be restored!

You mean, it's up to *me*?
But, what could I possibly do here?
Why, in my own little corner,
I am practically invisible!

Lord, may *my* peace be restored.
The peace in my own heart toward others.
Help me change—from fears and hatreds—to love.
Lord, may Your Peace be restored!

Conversations

Today I will have a hard conversation
With my Lord about His demands
Of my faithful obedience,
And my sense of His absence;
And what I expect of His actions.

I will listen to His promises,
And I will think about how I live,
My obedience and freedom,
And whom I will welcome.
And what He'll expect of my actions.

Lord, these issues will be difficult, at best,
Because I'm not sure how I feel.
Lord, I know I have sinned,
And been disobedient.
My actions will change, Lord, I promise!

Acquitted

The man walked into the courtroom.
A witness declared, "He's *guilty*!
Guilty of treason against God!
I heard him blaspheme,
And I heard him say
He doubted that God existed!

Then Jesus entered the courtroom
And softly announced, "'Twas for this I died."
The judge's ruling: Acquitted!

The woman entered the courtroom.
A witness arose; "She's guilty!
She's a thief, and a prostitute.
And these ugly sins have blackened her soul!
She should be judged by her fruits."

Others came into the courtroom.
Each one was told they were "guilty!"
This one had hatred of others,
This one led the mob that looted the stores,
And these persecuted police.

Then, Jesus entered the courtroom.
He proclaimed, "I have died for these also."
And the judge ruled, "All—acquitted!"

Goliath

The Israelites stood
In position for battle,
But they all were paralyzed.
They feared the challenge
Of the bully, Goliath.

How could one person
Stand up to such a warrior,
And still survive the battle?
Too much of a risk!
If they lost, the *nation* lost!

My question becomes,
What then is my Goliath?
What causes my quaking fears?
How can I survive?
If I lose, then evil wins.

Where is my David?
Who can stand for me and fight?
Jesus promised He's with me.
I must now believe—
Have faith in the unseen—God.

Different

To be "different" does not mean you're "wrong,"
It only means you are "other."
    When you have a different opinion,
You see things other than they do.
When you share love of Christ with others,
You're showing them a "different" way.

Say "Ahhhh"

The doctor probes and pokes at me,
Checking my physical condition.
Blood pressure and heartbeat,
Temp and reflexes,
"Breathe deep" and "Say ahhhh,"
Then pronounces me healthy.

God asks that I poke and I prod
To give myself Spiritual checkups.
What has priority,
Prayer life, and values,
Obey, be humble,
How's my devotional life?

Having salvation-forgiveness,
I will have confidence before God.
Humility wins souls.
Is my conscience clear?
Forgiving others,
I find my soul is healthy.

A Sin

A sin begins with thought
Niggling away in my head,
Mere whisper of an idea.
But if given a chance,
It festers and rots the soul
Until it develops and grows.
And then, through my actions,
Sin's desire is to *destroy*.
Remember, the sin doesn't care!
I'm cleansed by repentance;
In believing Your promise:

Resurrection was meant for me.

A Remnant

"The blasphemies of the world—
The rancor, grating on My ears—
Such a multitude of complaints!
My ancient soul needs soothing."

So speaks the God of Heaven,
The Father, Creator of all.
How long before His patience ends?
Will there be time to repent?

What will "repentance" look like?
Never would mere words be enough.
But, giving all, wholeheartedly,
Will show itself through actions.

Though blasphemies of the world
And the multitude of complaints
Will still remain, He will know
A remnant believes in Him.

Awareness of Presence

Let nothing disturb nor frighten you
Let all things be but passing moments.
God and His love remain forever,
May His quiet peace be within you.

Asking for "awareness of Presence"
Is a prayer He delights to answer.
God, speaking through His almighty works,
Reminds us that His Will *will* prevail.

Evil that lives in our wicked world
Succeeds, each time we give in to sin.
Each time we ask, He's willing to help
As we navigate this world of ours.

So ask for "awareness of Presence,"
And He'll gladly reside in your heart.
Each time you are tempted, remember!
Repent and receive His forgiveness.

The Loser

Judas! Even his name is hard to say!
He was such a loser.
Everyone says so.
He was a *thief*, you know.
He must have been obsessed with money;
Especially as "keeper of the purse."

Residual anger must still lie within,
To portray Judas so.
Judas, vilified,
And called "the Betrayer,"
When all he'd wanted was to get Jesus
To proclaim himself the Messiah!

Once he'd lived as "brother" to disciples.
Side by side, they'd traveled
Along with Jesus;
Together, as one flesh.
No *wonder* why he took his own life,
When brothers of his heart despised him

Lost Time

May I not return to the lost time—
All the years of not noticing You,
Of not seeing Who's right beside me;
Years of great difficulties,
Years of great opportunities—lost,
Of all the blessings I have missed—
Just because I was lost in time.

I know time "lost" cannot be restored.
All the time I thought I knew the way,
Yet not seeing Whose way I'd missed;
Lost in my difficulties,
Times of my own choosing to be lost,
Times of seeking pleasures elsewhere.
Lost in my own times, I missed Yours!

Although all that time of being lost—
I've repented and have returned *home*!
I'm now baptized in the Spirit,
In the light of Your holiness.
Has anyone seen a change in me?
For I'm no longer feeling lost,
Since You, my Shepherd, have found me

In Holy Presence

When did we lose it, O Lord?
When did we even notice
Your holy presence was gone
From here, in Your sanctuary?
We're here, in Your church—
But where, Lord, are You?

Our faithlessness was revealed
In valleys, where we've lingered
In our humiliation,
Instead, Lord, of our returning
To the mountaintop
Of holy presence.

How do we gain it again;
This holy presence of God?
If we will return, and stay
In Your covenant with us,
Lord, we will remain
In holy presence!

God Calls

If God will call, He will equip,
On-the-job training is yours, on request.
As you begin, He'll show you how;
If He has called you,
You *are* the right person!

To wring the most out of each day
You must learn to live with trust in your heart.
Trust that God knows your daily needs,
Trust God's loving-kindness,
And His call will be true!

Heart-Faith

Practice staying calm and sane
    In the middle of my chaos.
An accessible God
    Renders it possible.
It's a personal heart-faith.

On empty? Whose fault is that?
    I chose to pass by, to pass on!
In daily refueling,
    Through prayer and in worship,
Practice personal heart-faith.

Build up my personal faith,
    Choosing others above myself.
In serving the Savior,
    I'll find your salvation!
God is the God of promise!

What's Your Answer

The breeding place of evil
Is in the human heart—
Hate will never drive out hate,
Nor will force redress all wrongs.
Only love can change a heart,
And Jesus Christ *is* love.

If one would question Jesus
About unending love,
He'd say, "Of *course* I love you.
How could you hate your brother?"
As we are *all* God's children,
What would be your answer?

The Thirsty Earth

As You, Lord, care for this thirsty earth,
You send down Your rain to quench it.
And the thirsting earth drinks of the rain
Until it is overflowing.

As You, Lord, care for my thirsting soul,
You send Your Spirit to fill me.
And, as I drink my fill of Your love,
It will overflow to others.

And, as You care for *all* those who thirst,
Your love continues to guide me.
Whenever I notice one in need,
May Your love overflow through me.

End or Beginning

Each "ending" is also a "beginning."
Changing from old to the new grows our faith.
Clothed in His presence, to witness for Christ,
Brings His powerful mercy to others.

When something is ending, open your eyes.
Don't be discouraged if you do not see.
Whatever your doubt, stand up to your fears;
When fears fall away, true faith can begin.

A Bit Deeper

The Cross

Don't be the type of a Christian
Who touts, "Name it, and then claim it."
Be an "under the Cross" Christian.
The Cross is what has proven love,
Not the number of toys you have.

How has the Cross affected you?
Has your perception ever changed
How you would view another's sins?
Stop, don't evaluate others.
For the Lord says, "Judgment is Mine."

God has heard the cries of terror.
In sounds of dread, when peace should reign,
Christ hears the cries of His people.
He will restore and bring them home.
Compassion, proven by the Cross!

Don't Just Sit

Don't just sit, lamenting the lack
Of true worship in today's world.
Tell God's story in new spaces,
In places His word's not been heard.
Don't be surprised, God's there as well.

Go look for some answers
In unexpected places.
Don't let your gifts go dormant,
But use them, for His kingdom,
With songs of joy in your heart.

Do Not Doubt

Do not doubt;
Do not question
Nor complain of what He's doing
For, it's only when reviewing
That you'll see God's hand at work.

Do not doubt the Word of God,
For what He's promised—He will do!
You'll see, if you will read His word,
That He's the God of Promise!

Do not doubt the Lord, your God!
Don't question His understanding;
He knows everything about you,
And He loves you—anyway!

Another Experience

I've had another experience;
Another I'm not too sure about.
I have a couple questions to ask;
Was this experience meant for me,
To help me to grow even closer;
Or, was it meant to make me useful,
For You to use as an example?
If You sent me this experience
In order that I might become useful,
Did outcome show the needed changes?

Move Forward

Do not deny your sins,
But be responsible.
Learn, and then move forward
To what God has planned for you.

For if you "just" repent,
And cannot yet move on,
What can there be to life?
What's good about being stuck?

As you're moving onward,
Don't find new ways to sin;
Choose directions with care.
Which way will you go?

Time to Repent

Is there time to repent?
He could call at any moment.
I must stay alert,
I must be prepared
And "behave myself"
All the time!

For if a heart attack
Threatened, and I was to expire
That very moment
I profaned His Name,
Would there then be time
To repent?

For You

Don't look for loopholes,
Just freely accept
Gifts of His Spirit,
His grace—from His hand.
Unconditional,
His love is immense,
And mercy abides.
While still a sinner,
He came down—for you!

Priority One

I've got so much to do, Lord.
I've limited time and energy.
My life is finite, Lord,
I'll never get everything done!

Whoa!
May I remember, Lord,
To do the *first* things first!
Show me my true priority.
Do I really make You "Priority One"?

Me

When I decide to open the door,
Giving God complete access to me,
Then a life that's been drifting
And wasting away
Is reclaimed from a life filled with sin.

I realize that I cannot claim
That in life I'll not sin again,
But I'll proclaim my *desire*
To walk beside You,
And relinquish all rights to be "me."

The Reason

The reason you have been delayed
May be the protective hand of God.
You were not in that accident
Because of that delay on the road.

The reason you have been harmed
May be because God's merciful hand
Protected you from evil ways
That were intent of causing you pain.

The reason for the deadly disease
That's eating away inside of you
May be because of your own sin.
But He is there—you are not alone!

How Dare I?

"Lord, I call upon You.
Hasten to me!
Give ear to my voice when I call to You."*

How *dare* I!
Lord, You call down to me!
You ask me to listen to You!
I must listen for Your voice when You call to me!

How could such a prayer
Be "counted as incense before You"?*

But, Lord, "In You I take refuge,"*
For You, Lord, will never
Leave me to my own devices.
I would not be left defenseless,
I am NOT alone.

Lord, when I call upon You,
I beg You to listen to my cry.
I know You will hear me.
I know You will respond—in Your timing—
For this is why I was created.

*Psalm 141, NASB

The Shape of Waiting

What is the shape of waiting?
Is it triangular
For the Holy Trinity,
Of Father, Son, and Spirit?

What shape does waiting take?
Is it softly rounded
As a woman's fulfilled wish
With all pregnant hopes and dreams?

What is the shape of waiting?
Is it rectangular,
With sharp angles at each end,
Reminding us of wanting?

What is your shape of waiting?
And what shape *would* you take?
Is it different for each one,
To wait in fear or with hope?

Don't Even Try

Don't even try to contain the love,
This unabashed *joy* of knowing God!
Relationships are love, gushing forth,
Joy overwhelming, and peacefulness.
For we now live beyond our known lives;
Beyond circumstance surrounding us.
And now we love, becoming like Christ,
As we help others who are in need.

Don't even try to understand why
We have such pure joy in knowing God.
As we are learning to live our lives,
It's enough to know such love exists;
Enough to know God walks beside us
As He's guiding each step of our way.
And, as we now know, to love like Christ
Means walking with those who are in need.

January First

January first…and it is snowing
muffling the sounds of the world.
Tiny bullets of white, half-horizontal
piercing through gray
against white of house behind us.

Only color is the darker gray of trees
or beige of another home
or metallic red of decking.

White, grays, monochrome silence.

Peace

Jesus First

Not as a last resort;
No, turn to Him *first*!
Faith often guides you
    Around an obstacle.
But if God guided you to it,
    Faith helps you through.
Do not attempt anything
    Without first going to Him.
Stay in the arms of Jesus
Be drenched with the love of God!

As God Said

Samuel did as God said;
    He chose David
    And anointed him King.
David did as God said;
    He was a man
    After God's own heart.
The Psalmist did as God said;
    Entered the temple
    And worshipped his God.
The leper did as God said;
    Was healed as he went,
    Then returned to give thanks.
The blind man did as God said;
    He washed in the pool,
    And saw, for the first time.
When I do as God says,
    How will He change me?
    What will I see?

Jesus Asked Me

Jesus once asked Peter,
"Do you love Me?"
Peter answered, "Yes, Lord!
You know I love You!"
Likewise, Jesus asked me,
"Do you love Me?"
My *life* depends on Him!
How *else* to answer?

Jesus then asked Peter
To "feed My sheep."
By preaching Words of God,
Peter fed the flock.
How will I "feed" His sheep?
By promising
To live a worthy life;
Show love through action.

Half Enough

Unless the Lord will guard my soul,
It's useless, with no earthly good.
Unless I seek a thankful heart,
How could I teach another "Love"?
Unless my mind is set on God,
Why would He lead me on His path?
Unless I take a timely step
All my praise will never be
Even half enough.

When all my mind and heart and soul
Belong to Who created me—
That I be in relationship;
That I would love and serve my Lord—
Then all of me can't be enough
Unless I can accept the Cross.
Salvation comes through Christ alone,
And all my praise cannot be
Even half enough!

Insulted

A good friend mocked me,
Saying, "You're religious!
But that's quite OK."
I asked for Your patience.

Another friend thinks
Devotions are "silly,"
It's stupid, at best,
To have a "quiet place."

I've been insulted
Because I'm a Christian.
I *plan* to stand firm,
Whenever that happens.

If I am "accused"
Because I'm a
     Christian,
Help me remember
To smile and to praise You.

This kind of "trouble"
Because of my witness,
Is *pale* when compared
To the death of a martyr!

Risk

You realize, you must give up
Your tendency to play it safe,
For when you live a risk-free life
It is a form of disbelief.
What's known about the world you're in
Is more than you could comprehend,
For, underneath what's visible
Are mysteries you cannot see
Until the Lord will take you Home.
For, when you love the Lord, your God,
You then will know that all are called;
And you'll obey, no matter what.
You'll go through trials and any risk
To do what God has asked of you.

The Waters

God parted the waters of the Red Sea,
Saving His people from the Egyptians.
The Israelites then stepped forward in faith.
And God then destroyed enemy armies.

When people grumbled, God made the waters
Flow from the rock, as He had told Moses.
The people wandered between the waters
Until the Lord directed them forward.

After His people stepped forward in faith,
God parted waters of Jordan River,
Leading His people into the promise.
With God's help, they prospered in the land of Canaan.

What waters has the Lord parted for you?
How do you need to step forward in faith?
What does He ask you first to deliver
Before he blesses *new* waters for you?

Aimless

Nothing moves with aimless feet,
Because God has a plan for all.
The world seems to flow so thoughtlessly,
But *word*, when planted in your heart,
Will settle there, and bring forth fruit
That changes lives forever.

How do you handle weakness?
Why do you wander aimlessly
When Jesus Christ had died for you;
And He has risen from the dead
To prove to you God's love is real.
He wants to walk beside you.
If you choose to walk alone,
You need not walk with aimless feet;
The Savior calls, with hand held out,
"Get up, and walk, and come to Me."
By God's own power, we obey,
And choose to walk with Jesus.

Prepare the Way

John will prepare us, in order that we
Prepare the way for our Savior.
We begin by accepting
The fact of His coming,
And then by *expecting* arrival!

Out of the wilderness of all our doubts,
Out of our sins, our troubles, our trials,
We are called to repent,
And we're called to return,
To put all our love into *action*.

The voice in the wilderness, crying out,
"Prepare Ye the Way of the Lord Who Comes!"
The voice is so wistful.
Proclaiming His yearning.
His desire is for *all* to be saved.

A Turned-On Believer

Be a "Turned-On Believer"
Then people might ask,
"Just what *is* that scent you're wearing?"
Being "Tuned in" to Jesus
Means people will see
Just what it means to be Christian.

Whether "tuned in" or "turned on"
Others may join you
When they see how much you have changed.
When you're "easy" on others,
You're acting like Christ.
How has God's love seemed to change you?

When your love is apparent
You show you're chosen
For purpose of service to all.

For This Delights Him

Our "feelings" or our perception
Have naught to do with God's Presence.
He's ready to guide us to Truth,
For this delights Him.

When you think He's too far to hear,
Just whisper His name, He'll be there.
Open yourself to His Presence,
For this delights Him.

Life Answers

Are you looking for life's answers?
Do you even know the question?
Don't worry about another
For each person's path is unique.
Base faith on who God truly *is*,
Not just on what He's done for you.
Daily thankfulness will cushion
The impact of life's many trials.
Seek His heart, and delight in Him,
For He delights when you obey.

Death—Life

Death will enter into life
To teach us life is precious.
Something that is ours forever
Becomes insignificant fact.

Plant a seed in fertile ground,
Water carefully, and watch.
The seed must die 'ere plant can bloom,
And blooms must die 'ere seeds be formed.

To bear good fruit in our lives
We must die to sins within.
Accept as Savior, Jesus Christ,
And we will live our life for Him.

God's Acceptance

God's acceptance of you
Is not based on your "goodness"
You are always in God's own heart,
For God has said you are His delight!

You cannot become "good"
Without God's gift of His grace.
His grace is always sufficient
For everyone, including for you.

God loves each, equally,
And He will delight in each.
Far beyond merely "acceptance,"
God loves *you*. He's proved it through Jesus!

Jesus Rules

Don't focus on the storms,
Instead of on His story.
Do not abandon faith in Him
When the times of destruction appear.
Trust Him. Listen, and persevere,
False preachers proclaim a new age.
Remember: *Jesus* rules!

You Are My God

When we build walls of defense
Against the chaos of the world,
Against the hatred, the anger
Of those who despise us,
You, Lord, still love us.

Your salvation makes us safe,
Whatever is our circumstance.
If I'm deep in angry despair,
And I've turned to You,
You, Lord, are my God.

I'm not really unwilling
To open my heart to You, Lord.
My own little world intrigues me
And I often forget
That *You are* my God!

Rest Restores

In running to and fro,
Getting all in place,
I exhaust myself,
Forgetting: Rest Restores!
When mind flits here and there
Checking on my list,
Certain I forgot
All-important items,
My Lord God reminds me:
"Learn to lean on Me;
I can do all things;
Remember: Rest Restores."
Then, rested and restored,
Spirit in my heart
Guiding all I do…
I find *much* more gets done!

My Lines

My lines have been laid in pleasant places.
My heritage is beautiful to me!
Satan attacks us where we are weakest;
I'd once turned away, but since have returned.
Still did I trust Him when things appeared bleak.

God never turned from His great love for me.
There's been no "great trials" for me to endure,
Though life has had "blips," there's nothing desperate.
Should I be worried, should I be concerned
What alloy, what dross God still must remove?

God's Poem

The lines of your life
Are written in love.
You are God's workmanship!
You are God's poem.
He delights in you.

What does your poem
Say about your life?
Are you walking between
The lines of your faith?
Or are you clueless?

Incomplete poems,
Still being written,
Completed in Jesus.
God's activity
Will be shown in you.

Prior to gifting,
God knows how each line
Will fit with all others.
All work together
In those who love God.

Be Still and Know

"Be still, and know that I Am God"
(Ps. 46:10 NIV)

What on earth does it mean to "be still"?
Is it a physical quiet,
    Not fighting with frustration,
    But sitting still, not moving?
Is it emotional stillness,
    Not concerning self with problems,
    But calmness, and acceptance?
Is it a spiritual quiet,
    Not thinking of a future plan
    But focusing on Jesus?
Perhaps "be still" includes all of these.

What does it mean to know He is *God*?
Is it a physical knowing?
    Who but God could create a world
    And fill it with all we see?
Is it emotional knowing,
    When hearts are filled with brother-love,
    And when we help another?
Is it a spiritual knowing,
    When deep inside our hearts and souls
    We know, without a question,
That the Lord is *God*—and *we are not*.

Ponder Impossible

Ponder impossible
Of grace and God's mercy
Forgiving all sins
You have ever committed.

Ponder impossible,
Your sins are forgotten.
Don't let past problems
Cloud current conversations.

Ponder impossible
Of love never-ending,
Enfolding your heart
From birth to beyond the grave.

Ponder impossible.
More than you dare to ask
He's willing to give,
Because He's love incarnate!

Indispensable Weapon

Use God's indispensable weapon
To help prepare for troubles;
Read God's Word, then sit in His presence,
Be strong in the Word, and pray for strength,
Encouraging each other.

Use God's indispensable weapon
To help prepare you for life.
Read His Word, for that's all you will need.
But "community" will help you grow
Ever closer to the Lord.

Use God's indispensable weapon.
Read His Word, and you will find
The model of how to live your life
In harmony with one another,
In harmony with your God.

Lord, You Save Me

No matter how I see You, Lord,
As my rock, or as my shield;
As my stronghold, or my refuge;
Lord, You save me!

No matter what my "enemies"
From others, or from myself,
From things, or thoughts, or temptations;
Lord, You save me!

No matter what is going on,
As earthquakes, or tsunamis,
Because You find delight in me,
Lord, You save me!

Psalm 18:1–19

My Life as Prayer

Lord, may I live my life as prayer.
What will You say, what will I do?
Knowing my life is on the line,
I'm more likely to wait for You.

Accepting weakness as Your gift,
Helps me keep my plan tentative,
For then, Your far superior plan
Has a chance to succeed in me.

Lord, do I need to be reined in?
Or will I be allowed to fly?
Not by my will, nor by my way,
But my prayer is that You'll use me!

The Lord

To feel the love of the Father,
To perceive creation's beauty,
Be able to pray in His Church,
And to serve Him in His Kingdom—
This will I seek, before all else.

Jesus, the Son, in His glory,
Waits—with arms flung wide-open.
Waiting for you to embrace Him,
Waiting to grant His forgiveness.
O Lord, You take time to listen!

What Joy

God, the Father of us all,
Sent His eldest child,
His most holy and precious Son,
Down to men on earth
In order to die
That He might save
All God's other children—
Including those willing to kill
This, their Holy Brother, Jesus,
Upon that cross.

Though He died many years ago,
We still stab at His corpse—
As though we could make Him deader.
God, the Father, still forgives,
For even the "worst" of these
Is still His child.
When the evilest of men
Comes to his senses and repents,
And returns to the Father—
Oh, what *joy* in heaven!

Who Do You Say I Am?

In this world of ours,
Where depravity is commonplace;
Where *Christian* is a dirty word;
Where one group hates the "other"
And "others" shoulder all the blame;
Where crime rates soar, and justice seldom wins;
Where sexual innuendo
Will invade all the media;
My Lord will ask me, "Where do you stand, Child
And who do you say that I am?"

Can I declare, with Peter,
"You are the Christ, Son of the Living God"?
You, Christ, fulfill all prophecy;
You're the One who fills all hearts,
And heals all hurts the world has dealt me.
You are my sovereign.
You love me, more than any other can.
You are my soul's benefactor,
My heart's love, and my life's mentor.
This, Lord, is Who You are—and I am Yours!

Ahhh!

Invited

You have invited me to come—
　　With all my gaping emptiness!
　　With all my depression,
　　With all my deepest yearnings.
O Lord, I come! I kneel before You!

You have invited me to come—
　　To face the emptiness within,
　　To *fill* my emptiness with Your fullness,
　　To rejoice in my dependence!
O Lord, I come! I kneel before You!

You have invited me to come—
　　Taking my refuge in You,
　　For You are my salvation
　　When storms of life abound.
O Lord, I come! I kneel before You!

You have invited me to come—
　　To become one of Your faithful ones,
　　To allow Your work be done through me,
　　To offer You *all* that I am.
O Lord, I come! I kneel before You!

Make Your Choice

Make your choice today
To walk a brand-new way
Along a fresh trail,
And God just might reveal
Things you did not know.

Might not be "routine,"
But *choose* to be with God.
Through thoughts and actions,
Your loyalty is key
To follow His plan.

Before we were *born*,
God had a plan for us.
Not what *we* would do,
But what *God did*—for us!
Make your choice for Him.

The Next Moment

In the very next moment of life
Who will you say that you are?
How will your heart and spirit react
To each new circumstance?

Is your spirit growing within you?
Do you experience new faith?
Do you see God's wonder, His power,
When life's storms assail you?

Are you fearful of your next moment?
Do not fear, for God *is* there!
Trust Him, O child, for He *is* with you
In every "next moment."

Best Friends

In the song I will sing,
I'm "joint heirs with Jesus,"
But that's not how I feel,
For I'd prefer to shout
I'm *best friends* with Jesus,
For as we walk He'll take my hand,
And lead me where He wants to be.
In quiet and in solitude,
We sit, we speak, we merely *are*—
Together, best friends, forever.

We, Your People

We, Your people, are repentant
Of all foul words, and ugly acts,
Of all offensive thoughts we've held.
O Lord, do not remain angry.*

We, Your people, rejoice in You,
For You, O God, are in our midst.
We are glad, and shout our praise,
For You, Lord, have forgiven us.**

We, Your people, are Your lampstands,
Lighting the way through a dark world.
While living by Christ's example,
We are lights of Your holy love.

*Isaiah 64:9
**Zephaniah 3:14, 17a

God vs. Satan

God, as ruler, reigns in love.
    His call is "Love men" and "Men, *love!*"
Satan follows a dictatorship of force,
    Whose call is "Blast men away, in hatred!"

God's Gospel is the Good News of Truth;
    Of peace, and promise, and salvation.
Satan's goal is the Bad news of lies,
    Of war, and defection, of condemnation.

God's Presence is within each soul,
    To nurture, encourage, and calm us.
Satan's desire is to grab each soul
    Away from God, do discourage, and to rile us.

God vs. Satan—no true contest,
    For God's way is clearly the better!
Though Satan refuses to concede until death,
    God Himself helps us maneuver through life.

Who Upset the World?

Who has upset the world?
Well, I'd have to say
There have been more than one.
One who comes to mind
Is Martin Luther King,
With "I Have a Dream."
Now that was "upsetting,"
And we thank God for it!
If not for Mr. King,
What would the world be like?

Who has upset the world?
Some that "upset" us
Did it through evil ways.
Hitler comes to mind,
Annihilating Jews—
Just because he could!
That was purely evil.
Also, are the henchmen
Of every dictator
Who's ever ruled on earth.

Who has upset the world?
Do you understand,
While some "upsets" are good,
Others are evil.
How do we ever know
Which is for our good?
One who "upset" the world
Whose every act was love;
Who died, to give us life;
Was Christ, God's only Son.

Doubt

I once told the Lord, "I doubt!
With questions unanswered,
With inadequate feelings,
And fears for the future,
How can I trust You?"

Your word may be a challenge,
Sometimes as discipline,
Or as a comforting thought;
But I know that Your word
Is here, within me.

When my mind is set on You,
And not on my feelings;
When I place my trust in You,
Then am I comforted,
And I'm whole again.

I'll believe, with all my heart,
Your word has given hope.
Discipline, a way of life
For all who choose to serve
The Lord, as Master.

I Can't Understand

I can't understand Your love for me,
And yet, Your word tells me it's true.
I can't understand why I'd believe
Unending love was mine to live.
Lord, strengthen my faith, that I'll obey;
That I may shine, through light of Thine;
That Your truth be shone, Lord. Yours alone!

I can't understand a love like Yours.
Whatever I might think or do,
Lord, may my life always honor you;
May I reflect Your love and truth
In a way worthy of Your Good News.
Help me to understand Your heart,
That my life be witness of Your grace.

The Lord's Call

When the Lord calls you,
He remains faithful
To bring it to pass.

What is the difference
'Tween good and evil
But motivation?

Doing a good deed
Does not mean pure hearts
Were truly involved.

While standing in faith,
One can become proud
And be contemptuous.

God knows what's in hearts
Of men and women,
For He knows it *all*!

Listen to the Lord
To hear His calling,
Then ask for His help!

Truth

Work life of the Spirit
Into details of life,
Not merely ideas
Or just sentiments.
God's Truth trumps your feelings
And Truth trumps ideas.
Live life to the fullest
With head, heart, and love.

Daddy, Would You Come

Daddy, would you come running
To meet this prodigal child?
I know that I've deserted
Everything I once believed;
But, I have since repented,
And chose to journey back home,
Return to where I belong!

Daddy, would you come outside
When I've refused to enter
The joyful celebration?
I find I can't forgive him,
This brother that I once loved.
I've chosen to stay outside,
Instead of where I belong.

Do For

Do for the least of these:
The hungry, the thirsty,
The stranger, the naked;
Do for those who are ill,
And all imprisoned souls,
As doing all, just for Me.

Do for the weak, and fearful,
Downtrodden, and depressed;
Do for the homeless man,
And those marginalized.
Remember, do these things
For your ever-loving God.

Your Mercy and Grace

Why have You led me here, O Lord,
To this barren, arid landscape
Which will bruise and disorient me?
Is it because both desert and cross,
Devoid of human possibilities,
Best portray Your mercy, Your grace?

As You lead me to this place, Lord,
Help me to perceive the blessings.
May I see the blessings given,
In pain or failure. Help me to trust
That these things are new opportunities,
Bringing to light Your mercy and grace.

May every humbling circumstance,
May each time I feel bewildered
Because my dreams are shattered and gone,
Bring me ever closer to Your heart.
Awaken me from slumber of routines.
Remind me of Your mercy and grace.

Your mercy and Your grace, O Lord,
Are all I have to keep me sane;
For long ago I learned to focus
Upon Your love, so freely given.
And now, Your peace that sings, that burns within,
Is mine forever—if I'll believe.

Paul

(Barclay / Romans)

The sins of human nature
Were but "challenges" to Paul.
Aware of evil,
He's just as aware
Of great, redeeming
Power of Christ, to save us.
None was "too bad" to be saved!

Hard Times or Good

While you are not "made" by hard times you've had,
How you get through them is quite revealing.
Are you now bitter, and seek to destroy?
Or did you forgive and seek to bless them?

We all make choices, each day of our lives.
The choices we make seem to define us.
Choose to be grateful, sing praise to the King.
Seems "good times" reward those choosing to love.

Be Prepared

An accident and a blessing
Each can (and will) change your life.
It's how you will prepare for them
That will determine impact.

When unprepared, an accident
Can cause bitterness and strife.
When prepared, you can better cope
Because God is on your side.

When unprepared, any blessing
Can also catch you off guard.
You'll be unable to handle
Those blessings that come your way.

How to prepare is the question.
Dig wells before droughts arrive;
Immerse yourself in God's Scriptures,
His *Word* will guide all actions.

Two Other Crosses

Two other crosses stood there on that hill,
Each representing God's gift of choice.
One man chose death, the other chose life.
We have been granted the same choice as they.
All your bad choices, redeemed by the one.

Two other crosses, silently standing,
Prove we have choices: to die or live.
With each bad choice redeemed by Jesus,
Will you die unredeemed, or live in love?
Make your choice to live through His living grace!

Gifts I Bear

In deep silence,
Levels of intimacy
Need no words,
For God hears our silent plea
To bear all our sins away.

When I am "real,"
True to myself before God,
I allow Him
To bring forth the very gifts
He planted deep in my soul.

The gifts I bear
Deeply hidden in my soul
Are tightly held
Until Jesus speaks them free,
Releasing them to the world.

The *best* in me,
Given to me at my birth,
Is not enough
Unless the center is Christ.
Then all will flow forth freely

His Faithful Love

They will see in our history, the faithful love of the Lord.
(Ps. 107:43, NLT)

What will they see, what will I tell?
How has the Lord shown His faithful love?
When did it start, why did He care?
Whose life have I impacted,
Showing His love?

Way back in the womb it began.
He cared. I am one of His children.
His love's portrayed in life and death
Of Jesus Christ, my Savior,
Who died for me.

In my personal history,
Mom and Dad brought me to Sunday school.
But adolescence bred disdain.
Turning my back on Jesus,
I became lost.

As a young adult, I neglected
To insist our child attend the church.
At least he was confirmed, thank God.
And therefore, seeds were planted
He had a chance.

Not giving in, God opened up
My heart, my life, to worship again.
Forgiving me for sinful ways,
His faithful love convinced me
    That I am His!

Have I impacted anyone?
Through my stories and my poetry
I hope to show his faithful love,
Thereby convincing others
    To live in Him.

Hope, Joy, and Happiness

It's hope that whispers in my ear,
So gently that I cease to hear
The clashing, rumblings of this earth
That still attempt to distract me.

It's joy of God that speaks to me
No matter where I'm found to be
When I will listen for His voice;
And God, Himself, be my Dear Friend.

What happiness is mine this day
That when I knelt right here to pray
I heard His voice, so clearly say,
"My child, you know you're My delight."

I Will Serve

I will serve God—
Not because I must,
But I must serve
Because I love Him!

You Hem Me In

O Lord, You hem me in.
You are beside and alongside me.
You lead me from before me,
And you push me from behind.
You are above and beyond me!

You lead, with righteousness and justice.
You remain with me as I show
My brokenness, my failures.
With Your steadfast love, You guide
When I stumble, and I falter.

Do You intend to hide from me
I yearn for Your love, o Lord!
When rejected and remorseful,
When I repent, I know You'll accept,
And I'll ever sing your praises.

I will exalt, O God, I will praise.
I choose to love You with all my heart,
Encourage and celebrate each life.
And, with the Psalmist, I will sing—
"Blessed be the name of the Lord!"

In the Now

I am with you in every "now"
As I'll be with you in each "then."
Be in the present moment.
Enjoy peace in My presence.
I, Myself, promise to redeem
Whoever won't quench My Spirit.

Each day can become a "good day,"
For My presence permeates time.
You see things as in the "now,"
I see them as they can be.
If you would see things through My eyes,
Together we could change your life.

What is the size of your problem?
Are you unwilling to trust Me?
The more challenging your day,
The more power I can give.
My power's at your disposal
Whenever you depend on Me.

God's Gifts

Jesus Christ was rejected by many
At the same time, He brought joy to others.
How could I tell them, what would I say?
What would convince them to listen. O Lord?

The deepest thoughts in our hearts are revealed
By how we respond to the gifts of God.
God's gift of mercy, the gift of God's grace;
We could not *dream* of anything better!

There's a huge difference between our sins
And God's great gift of forgiveness
We can't earn, or win, anything from God,
So—receive God's gifts, or do without them.

Before It Began

Before the beginning of the world,
God prepared the kingdom for me.
He promised that I would inherit,
And live with Him in His heaven.

Before I was born, God knew my form;
He alone knit me together.
He took a skein from both Mom and Dad,
And formed the unique design.

Before I began to talk or to walk,
God understood the route I'd take.
He knew what I'd say and what I'd do;
He also knew I would return.

Before I repented of my sin
God knew me, and still He loved me.
Now that I have returned to His fold,
I'm aware: He'd *always* been there!

Egypt

There must be a soft spot
In the heart of God
For Egypt.

It was to Egypt Abraham journeyed,
Escaping the draught in Canaan.
God called him out when it was safe
To return to the Land of Promise.

It was to Egypt God's people fled,
Escaping hunger during draught
Of their own land.
There they remained,
Until God called them out
To return and to conquer Canaan.

It was to Egypt Joseph fled,
Escaping Herod's pursuit
In the spiritual draught
Within their own land.
There they remained
Until God called them out,
As foreseen in Scripture,
When it was safe once again.

There must be a soft spot
In the heart of God
For Egypt.

Foundation of Grace

The foundation of grace
In a believer's heart,
Can become undermined
By guilt-evoking words.
Don't build a tunnel, build bridges.

The foundation of grace,
A God-given blessing,
Is to be encouraged
By love-inspired words.
Build bridges by helping others.

The Will

In finding the will
> To will the Will of God,
There we discover
> A child of the Father
> Loves living as Jesus.

Are we committed,
> Or merely complacent?
To live in His will
> As child of the Father
> Demands our commitment.

Share the Blessing

Is there a cry that none can hear?
A cry of pain or anguish?
Whoever cries, the Lord responds
Through his overwhelming grace.

All are but flawed, chipped jars of clay,
But God has washed and cleansed us
To hold again His loving grace.
Refilled, we feed another.

Therefore, that cry none seemed to hear,
God sent us there, to listen.
As we've been saved through love of Christ,
We are to share this blessing.

Lush and Lovely

A life that's lush and lovely
Has a certain quietude.
The times I have with Jesus,
Away from this world's troubles,
Means everything to me.

A life of useful meaning
Should first begin with Jesus.
How else could you recover
From this world's evil problems
If you were not prepared?

A life that's lush and lovely
Is yours, just for the asking.
Jesus Christ will walk with you,
He will guide your every step.
He's waiting for you now.

The Design

The Almighty made the design.
We are handcrafted by God!
Not only did He make the mold,
He wants to live within us.

You celebrated my return
Each time that I repented.
The only "Now" I want to know
Is the Joy of Heaven's song.

O Lord of Love, You're still with me
When I awake each morning.
From the design until the end,
You're here, with each step I take.

Joy of the Lord

Joy of the Lord exists within
Subtle happiness, inner peace;
In smiling hearts and quiet souls.
This joy comes from our knowing Christ
This Christ, who died for each one's sins.
But, even more, He brings us hope—
Hopes for eternal tomorrows.
The joy of Christ gives lasting peace,
Happiness, and sweetness of life!

My Last Breath

(Ps. 104:33–34, NLT)

"I'll sing to the Lord as long as I live.
I will praise God to my very last breath!"
I'll seek to please Him, and I'll seek to serve.
Wherever Your need, Lord, please, just send me.

Though all temptations try to derail me,
Lord, in Your mercy, hold tightly to me!
Don't let despair, anxious feelings, or fears,
Cause me to turn and refuse You my heart!

I will let trust and thankfulness guard me.
I'll not allow fear to gain an entry.
Then I'll be free to sing with each heartbeat,
Praising my God to my very last breath.

The Empty Tomb

"Early, while it was yet dark,"
They went to visit the tomb.
(Would I have gone? Did I attend?)
And once the disciples
Saw the tomb was empty,
What did they do? They went home!
Would I have merely shrugged,
As in, "Oh, He's gone? OK."
Would I then turn, and go home?

The Elders cautioned Pilate,
"Make sure His tomb is secure!"
So, then, Pilate sent a few guards?
Did he fear that the dead
Would no longer be dead?
How could guards secure the world
Against a miracle?
Lord, with you, there is nothing—
Nothing that's impossible!

Faithful

Faith of the prayerful
    Releases the *Word* on the world.
Pray that the Father
    Will grant to the nations a peace,
        Surpassing all hopes.

Prayers of the faithful,
    Praying for enmity to end.
Waiting for promise
    Beating the swords into ploughshares…
        When dare we begin?

Gifts

With gift of roots
To anchor me
Through heredity.
I know who I am.
Your gift of roots
Will hold me fast.
I'll travel the path
You've laid out for me.

With gift of wings
To fly away,
I will choose to stay.
I know whose I am.
Your gift of wings
Will let me go…
Allow me to soar
And fly to my Lord.

Looking Back

When they, way in the future,
Pause and look into their past,
When they see our names before them,
May they follow where we've gone.

May our testimonies for You
Be such that moves them forward.
May our lives be their true signposts
To the Savior that we love.

Hush, Child, Hush

Hush, child, hush.
Let Me get a word in edgewise.
Hush your thoughts,
Calm your actions,
Quiet your soul,
And listen to Me.

Hush, child, hush.
Let Me speak My word within you.
Let My thoughts
Become the acts
That can prove My love.

Hush, child, hush.
Remember the truth of My love.
I love you.
So, let this truth
Become enough
To quiet your heart.

Music of Heaven

All pieces of the universe,
The dislocated, the broken,
The Cross of Christ restores them all
To sing in vibrant harmonies
The tuneful music of Heaven.

In learning more of how God works,
How He forgives us all, in love,
How, from beginning to the end
He towers over everything,
We learn to sing Heaven's music.

Grounded and steady in our trust
Of Jesus, our loving Savior,
We'll then learn how to do our work,
Help and love others as ourselves,
And sing the music of Heaven.

Handcrafted

I have been handcrafted.
The Potter took the clay
And molded it by hand.
He formed the flow of life,
And when He claimed it "done,"
He sent me into the world.

From in my mother's womb
The Father knew my form.
Before my life began,
He knew each turn I'd take.
He knows I would return
And praises would fill my heart.

Handcrafted by the Lord!
O, what a loving thought,
That He would take the clay
And form me as His child!
I can but praise the Lord
For blessings He has given!

No Darkness

There is no darkness
That His Light cannot reach.
There is no sin
His forgiveness will not cleanse.
There is no slavery
That His Life has not set free.
There is no life
That His does not enrich!

Amen

God comes, and meets with me
In sacred places
And in intimate spaces
    Of my life.

The Lord of the Universe,
He who created all that I know,
He is the One who watches over me.
He is my Guard, and my Delight.

Do I really thank Him
    For everything?
For the huff and puff? For aches and pains?
For snows piled high, autumnal rains,
For scorching heat, or bitter cold?

But if I thanked Him not for these,
How could I praise the gentle breeze?
How could I thank Him for the Word,
For daily gifts of exceptional love
Abundantly given, plus more again?
Dear Lord, I thank You now. Amen.

A Bit Deeper

At Home with God

Slip into the center
Where your soul is at rest
Beyond the strain
To peace and joy,
At home,
    With God.

Printed by Libri Plureos GmbH in Hamburg, Germany